ISAAC NEWTON

First published in North America in 2007 by the
National Geographic Society
1145 17th Street N.W.
Washington, D.C. 20036-4688

Trade ISBN: 978-1-4263-0114-8
Library ISBN: 978-1-4263-0115-5
Library of Congress Cataloging-in-Publication Data available on request.

Originated in Hong Kong by Modern Age
Printed and bound in China by Midas Printing Limited

Publisher: Richard Green
Commissioning editor: Claudia Martin
Art direction: Ivo Marloh
Picture manager: Veneta Bullen
Production: Anna Pauletti

Consultant: Dr. Rob Iliffe
Design and editorial: Tall Tree Ltd.
Picture research: Caroline Wood

For the National Geographic Society:
Project editor: Virginia Ann Koeth
Art director: Bea Jackson

Previous page: A reconstruction of Newton's work table at Trinity College, Cambridge: a prism, an astrolabe, and tables of logarithms can be seen.
Opposite: This medal in memory of Isaac Newton was issued in 1727.

ISAAC NEWTON

THE SCIENTIST WHO CHANGED EVERYTHING

PHILIP STEELE

NATIONAL GEOGRAPHIC

WASHINGTON, D.C.

CONTENTS

YOUNG ISAAC

1

FIRED BY GENIUS

2

SECRETS OF THE UNIVERSE

3

MAN OF THE WORLD

4

YOUNG ISAAC

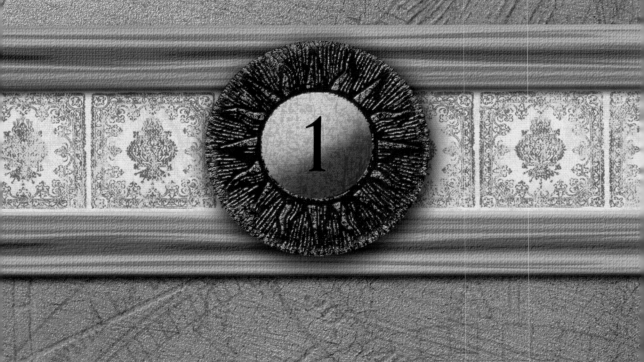

1

Born in Midwinter

It was two o'clock in the morning and it was dark and bitterly cold. The date was a special one—December 25, 1642. It would be a strange Christmas this year: King Charles I was at war with the English Parliament and a civil war was raging throughout the country. These were troubled times in England.

At Woolsthorpe Manor the windows were bright with candles and firelight, but this had nothing to do with Christmas. Nor were soldiers there with lanterns, demanding lodging for the night, as sometimes happened in those days. The reason why people were up at such an hour soon became clear, as the cry of a newborn child rang out from the upstairs bedroom. It was a boy, who had arrived early and was looking weak and sickly. In fact, he was so small that, as he said in later life, he could have fitted "into a quart pot," which measured about 2 pints (1.5 liters).

The owner of Woolsthorpe Manor, and the baby's father, had been an independent farmer named Isaac Newton.

When was Christmas?

Before 1582, all of Europe used the same calendar. However, in that year the Catholic Church brought in a new system of calculating dates. These changes were not adopted in Protestant countries until much later—in England, not until 1752. So December 25, 1642, would actually be January 4, 1643, by today's calendar.

Previous page: An illustration of a man flying a kite from John Bate's 1635 book, *The Mysteries of Nature and Art*. When he was a boy, Isaac made several kites from his own designs.

January 8, 1642

The great scientist Galileo Galilei dies in Italy.

August 1642

Civil war breaks out in England between King Charles I and Parliament.

Sadly Isaac Newton had died in October 1642, just before his son was born. Isaac had been a prosperous man of some standing in the neighborhood, but like most farmers he could not read or write.

The baby's mother was called Hannah. She came from a higher social class than her husband. Her brother, William Ayscough, was a clergyman who lived in the nearby village of Burton Coggles. William was an educated gentleman, who had studied at Cambridge University. The baby was baptized on the first day of the New Year, 1643. He was given his father's name, Isaac Newton.

Below: This is how Woolsthorpe Manor appeared in the 19th century. It still looks much the same today. Traditionally a manor house was the largest and most important house in any English village.

October **1642**

Isaac Newton (Senior) falls ill and dies.

December **25, 1642**

Isaac Newton (Junior) is born at Woolsthorpe Manor, Lincolnshire.

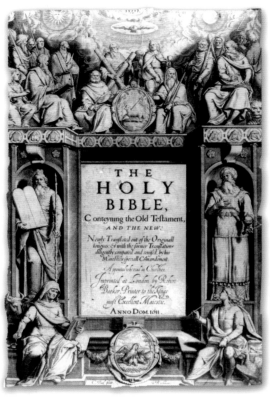

Left: In the 17th century, the Bible was read daily in church and at home. It was studied at school and was the only book many people came across.

The younger Isaac Newton was born in the same year that the great Italian scientist Galileo Galilei (1564–1642) died. Galileo had argued that the Earth revolved around the sun, rather than the other way around. Isaac, too, would grow up to be one of the greatest scientists ever born. But in Woolsthorpe nobody knew much about science, nor of an Italian named Galileo.

Woolsthorpe was a very small village near Colsterworth, in the eastern county of Lincolnshire, some 100 miles (160 km) north of London. Much of the county was made up of low-lying, waterlogged flatlands, known as the Fens. In northern Lincolnshire, the ground was higher, rising to green hills called Wolds. Woolsthorpe lay on a plateau in the west of the county, surrounded by farmland. It was near the highway which ran from London to York, which had been one of the most important trade and travel routes in Britain since Roman times.

The first years of Isaac's life were peaceful enough, although the civil war cast a shadow over everyday life throughout England. In 1643, Lincolnshire fell into the hands of the Parliamentary army.

January 1, 1643
Isaac Newton is baptized, probably at Woolsthorpe Manor.

July 2, 1644
A major defeat of Royalist forces by the Parliamentary army takes place at the Battle of Marston Moor.

Left: A country woman spins yarn at her wheel. Villages produced many of the items needed for daily life in England, such as cloth and food. Power was often provided by waterwheels or windmills.

When Isaac was three years old, in January 1646, his mother decided to marry again. Her new husband was a clergyman named Barnabas Smith. Smith was already 63 years old and was a wealthy man. He had no interest at all in young Isaac and was neither kind nor friendly.

Hannah moved away to live with her new husband at North Witham, about a mile and a half (2 km) from Woolsthorpe. It was decided that Isaac would be left behind at Woolsthorpe Manor. He would be looked after by his grandmother, Margery Ayscough, Hannah's mother. Isaac felt abandoned and desperately lonely. He had never known his father, and now his mother had left him as well. He was full of rage, and this anger seems to have smoldered inside him throughout his life. When Isaac was older, he confessed that he had threatened to burn down the house of his mother and stepfather over their heads.

The loner
Some modern experts have wondered whether Isaac Newton had a condition now known as Asperger's syndrome (AS). People with AS are often extremely intelligent but have trouble getting along with other people. Other experts argue that Isaac was just a loner, someone who found it difficult to make friends.

January 1646
Isaac's mother Hannah Newton decides to remarry.

1646
Isaac Newton stays at Woolsthorpe, in the care of his grandmother.

The World Turned Upside Down

An English popular song of 1643 was called "The World Turned Upside Down." Isaac Newton lived through a period of history when all the old values seemed to be overturned. New technologies were being developed. Printing presses produced large numbers of pamphlets inexpensively, rapidly spreading new ideas about religion and politics. There was religious conflict in many parts of Europe. Catholics battled with Protestants, and new religious sects were formed. Merchants and small landowners were becoming richer and wanted political power. They challenged the power of the nobles and kings.

Beginning in the 1620s, all these issues came to a head in Britain. King Charles I tried to break the power of Parliament, and in 1642 a civil war broke out between Royalists and Parliamentarians. Many of the Parliamentarians were extreme Protestants known as Puritans. The king was defeated, and in 1649 England became a republic or "Commonwealth." In 1653, power was handed over to the Parliamentarian leader Oliver Cromwell, who became a sort of dictator with the title "Lord Protector."

North Sea

SCOTLAND

Irish Sea

ENGLAND

Grantham
Woolsthorpe
WALES
Norwich
Cambridge

London
Dover
English Channel

Above: Great Britain was beginning to join together as a single nation. Wales and England were united by 1536, and shared the same ruler as Scotland from 1603. Full union was brought about in 1707.

Left: New nations were growing up in Europe. They founded colonies in the Americas and competed for trade. The Dutch and the English went to war in 1652–54, in 1664–67, and again in 1672–74.

Above: Following his defeat, King Charles I was publicly executed in London in January 1649. As it was widely believed that kings ruled with the authority of God, this event sent shockwaves through Europe. The monarchy was restored in England in 1660, under King Charles II, but its powers became increasingly limited.

Left: Soldiers became a familiar sight in the English countryside during the violent wars of the 17th century.

From Day to Day

Village life was simple and practical in the 1640s. Children were expected to work hard and be helpful and obedient. Most people expected that Isaac would grow up to be a farmer like his father before him, but the well-educated Ayscoughs made sure that he also received an education.

Young Isaac was sent off to small day classes in nearby villages, where he learned to read, write, and count. He attended church every Sunday and listened to readings from the Bible.

Woolsthorpe Manor had been owned by the Newton family since 1623. It was an attractive, simple building made of local limestone. Isaac's bedroom was upstairs on the second floor.

At about the age of six, Isaac would have stopped wearing the long tunic (or "petticoats") worn by infants, and been given a doublet (a kind of jacket) and breeches. Cloth was of wool or linen.

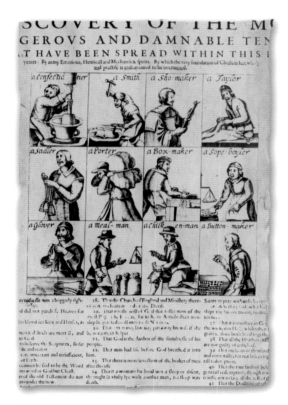

Above: Young Isaac Newton would have seen tradesmen such as these going about their everyday business.

1647–52
Isaac's mother, Hannah Newton, gives birth to three more children in North Witham.

January 30, 1649
King Charles I is executed in Whitehall, London.

Who banned Christmas puddings?

The Puritans were very serious people who thought that having fun was ungodly. During the Commonwealth period, they banned games of cards and dancing on the village green. They even stopped people from enjoying their traditional Christmas puddings.

Adults dressed simply during this time. The ribbons, frills, and lace worn by both men and women during the Royalist period were frowned upon by the Puritans. Instead, they preferred to wear plain and simple fashions in dark colors. Men were dressed in jackets and knee-length breeches, with stockings, broad collars, and wide-brimmed hats. Women wore long dresses as well as long, flat collars and aprons. Hooded cloaks were worn outdoors to protect against cold and wet weather.

Food was generally simple in the countryside, too. Woolsthorpe Manor farm would have provided milk and homemade butter, home-baked bread, apples, and eggs. It was difficult to feed livestock through the winter, so many cattle, sheep, and pigs were killed off each autumn. Meat and fish could be preserved in salt. Vegetables were more varied and of better quality than they had been a hundred years earlier. Beer was thought to be safer to drink than the water, which could be polluted with bacteria and disease. "Small" (weak) beer was even given to children.

Public health was poor. Many children died at a young age, and many women died in childbirth. Doctors used treatments that appear very strange to us today. They bled their patients with leeches, believing this made them well, and often handed out useless potions and ointments.

March 16, 1649
England becomes a Commonwealth, or republic.

July 8, 1652
A long series of wars between England and the Netherlands begins.

Isaac's Schooldays

In 1653, Barnabas Smith died and Hannah returned home. Isaac at last had his mother back at Woolsthorpe Manor, but he did not have her to himself. She had given birth to three more children. Isaac now had two half-sisters, called Mary and Hannah, and a half-brother called Benjamin.

In 1654 or 1655, Isaac was sent off to a boys' school in Grantham. This busy market town lay about 8 miles (12 km) to the north of Woolsthorpe. Isaac could not travel that far every day, so he boarded in a house on Grantham's main street. The building was the home of the town's apothecary, whom today we would call a pharmacist. He was a man named William Clark.

Isaac shared rooms with Mr. Clark's step-children, Edward, Arthur, and Catherine Storer. Isaac thoroughly disliked the boys, but he was friends with the girl.

Right: Apothecaries were forever mixing up potions, powders, ointments, and herbal remedies. It was probably at Clark's that Isaac gained an early interest in mixing up substances and observing how they reacted with each other.

August 1653
Isaac's mother returns to Woolsthorpe Manor.

December 1653
Oliver Cromwell is made Lord Protector.

He even made doll's furniture for Catherine. It was later suggested that, when they were older children, these two became sweethearts, but as an adult Isaac never had a girlfriend and would never marry.

Above: Isaac Newton carved his name on a windowsill and desks at the King's School.

The King's School in Grantham was one of the many free grammar schools that were founded all over England in the 16th and 17th centuries. School hours were long and dull, and much of the information was simply learned by heart. Beatings were frequent. Even so, English grammar schools did produce many great scholars in these years. The "grammar" referred to was Latin, not English. Latin, the language of the ancient Romans, was still used by scholars and scientists all over Europe, so learning it served a purpose. Pupils were also taught some Greek and Hebrew, for studying the Bible, as well as some arithmetic.

> *"... a sober, silent, thinking lad... never was known scarce to play with the boys abroad..."*
>
> **Catherine Storer recalls Isaac Newton in Grantham**

1654–55
Isaac is sent to the King's School, Grantham.

1656
Dutch scientist Christiaan Huygens makes an accurate pendulum clock.

Right: Isaac had long been fascinated by sundials and shadows. He carved this sundial, which may be seen at Colsterworth Church, at the age of nine.

NEWTON: AGED 9 YEARS CUT WITH HIS PENKNIFE THIS DIAL. THE STONE WAS GIVEN BY C·TURNOR ESQ. AND PLACED HERE AT THE COST OF THE RT HON SIR WILLIAM ERLE A COLLATERAL DESCENDENT OF NEWTON. 1877.

Isaac was unpopular and he was often bullied by other boys at the King's School. One day his patience snapped and he fought back furiously, smashing his tormentor's face into the churchyard wall. The fight certainly made Isaac no friends.

Isaac found his lessons dull, and at first he seems to have failed to impress the headmaster, Henry Stokes. However, Isaac's mind had already started to race ahead. The boy borrowed books from the library in the church. One of them was called *The Mysteries of Nature and Art* by John Bate. It was full of machines and contraptions.

Now Isaac began to make his own working models of windmills and all sorts of other ingenious gadgets, including mousetraps, water clocks, and kites that carried lanterns. Mr. Stokes at last began to realize that he had a very special pupil on his hands.

However, Isaac's mother Hannah did not recognize her son's special talents. In the fall of 1659, she took her son out of school. She thought it was time for the 16-year-old to learn more about farming, so he returned to Woolsthorpe Manor.

September 3, 1658
Oliver Cromwell dies.

1659
Isaac Newton is taken out of school to try his hand at farming.

However, Isaac proved to be completely useless as a farm manager. He was fined for letting his pigs and sheep stray, and for failing to keep his fences in good repair. His uncle, William Ayscough, and schoolmaster, Henry Stokes, both agreed that, if Isaac were sent to a university, it would be better for him and better for the farm. Isaac was sent back to Grantham to finish school, and now boarded with Stokes.

Storm force

Isaac Newton later recalled his first scientific experiment, when he tried to measure the force of the wind. It was during a great storm that became famous because it occurred on the day that Oliver Cromwell died, September 3, 1658.

Below: The King's School in Grantham had several dozen pupils in Isaac's day. Schoolmaster Henry Stokes realized that the young lad should go on to study at Cambridge University.

May 8, 1660
The Restoration of the monarchy: Charles I's son becomes king as Charles II.

Autumn 1660
Isaac Newton returns to King's School, Grantham.

FIRED BY GENIUS

2

College Days

Since the Middle Ages, the buildings of Cambridge University had risen next to the River Cam, about 60 miles (100 km) south of Isaac's home. One of the university's best colleges was Trinity, which had been founded by Henry VIII in 1546. It was at this great institution that Isaac was enrolled, on June 5, 1661.

Cambridge University had gone through difficult times during the civil war. Royalists had lost their jobs. Now King Charles II, Charles I's son, was on the throne, and it was the Puritans who had to be careful about what they said or wrote. Young Isaac was something of a Puritan at heart. Although he occasionally went to taverns, he never got into drunken fights like some of the other students. He was full of religious anxieties and slow to make friends.

Students were classed into various groups. At the top were the privileged nobles, then the ordinary students or "pensioners."

Right: Many fine buildings surrounded Trinity College's Great Court and fountain. Isaac lived in Cambridge for most of the time until 1696.

Previous page: A portrait shows Isaac Newton as a young man at Cambridge.

June 5, 1661
Isaac Newton enrolls at Trinity College, Cambridge.

July 1662
The Royal Society, an academy of sciences, is chartered in London.

A true story?

One account of Newton's life suggested that he performed poorly at Cambridge, and that at graduation he was awarded what would now be called third-class honors, rather than first class. Perhaps this was because he was working on his own projects —or perhaps the story is untrue.

The lowest class of students were the "subsizars," who had to act as servants to other students in order to pay for their studies. Isaac was in this lowest group, because his mother did not want to pay his fees.

Isaac was expected to start his studies in the traditional way, by studying ancient Greek philosophers such as Aristotle (384–322 B.C.).

He worked hard, but it was not until his third year that he really came into his own. He began to read other ancient philosophers and also contemporary thinkers, such as Galileo Galilei. Isaac applied his mind to the great questions of science and tried to find answers. He set up experiments in his rooms, using contemporary scientific methods of observation and measurement.

He took up mathematics, filling notebooks with figures and diagrams. In April 1664, Isaac was appointed a scholar, which meant that he received a scholarship. In January 1665, he received his bachelor's degree, graduating in April of that year. With his scholarship, he could now afford to stay on at Cambridge and continue his research.

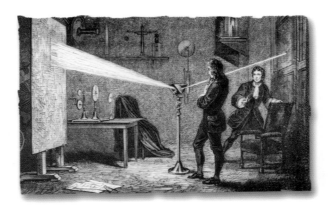

Right: Isaac Newton shared his rooms at Trinity College with a student called John Wickins. John helped Isaac set up experiments with light.

April 1664
Isaac Newton is made a scholar of Trinity College.

February 1665
Isaac Newton works on mathematics, including the "binomial theorem."

The Borders of Knowledge

The overthrow of the king in England marked the start of a social revolution. However, another kind of revolution was also under way in Europe. It was a revolution of ideas. These new ideas would completely change people's understanding of the world around them and its place in the universe. This was the beginning of modern science, although at that time people called it "natural philosophy." The word "scientist" was not used until the 19th century.

The ideas of ancient Greeks such as Aristotle, which had been accepted for 2,000 years, were now being challenged. A Polish astronomer called Nicolaus Copernicus (1473–1543) was even bold enough to suggest that the Earth traveled around the sun—a shocking idea at the time. European scholars now began to study the stars, planets, and the Earth, and the structure and motion of things. The language they used to describe their discoveries was mathematics.

As Newton came across the research of these modern natural philosophers his mind took flight. With their help, this awkward, irritable, and nervous young man entered a world of beauty and brilliance, in which his task was to search for the truth.

Above: Tycho Brahe (1546–1601) was a Danish astronomer whose detailed studies of the stars helped a German astronomer called Johannes Kepler (1571–1630) prove the truth about Copernicus' theory.

Right: Galileo Galilei was a brilliant Italian scientist who studied motion and the way in which objects fall to Earth. Galileo also made use of a new invention, the telescope, to observe the moon, the planets, and stars. His support for Copernicus' theory caused trouble with the Roman Catholic Church, which believed the sun moved around the Earth.

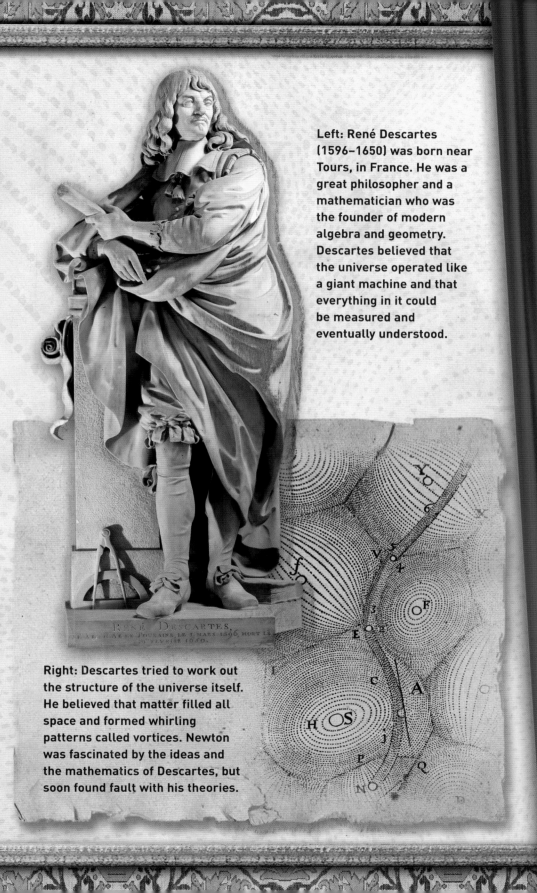

Left: René Descartes (1596–1650) was born near Tours, in France. He was a great philosopher and a mathematician who was the founder of modern algebra and geometry. Descartes believed that the universe operated like a giant machine and that everything in it could be measured and eventually understood.

RENÉ DESCARTES,
NÉ A LA HAVE EN TOURAINE, LE 1 MARS 1596, MORT LE
11 FÉVRIER 1650.

Right: Descartes tried to work out the structure of the universe itself. He believed that matter filled all space and formed whirling patterns called vortices. Newton was fascinated by the ideas and the mathematics of Descartes, but soon found fault with his theories.

The Crucible

A crucible is a dish used to heat metals or other substances to high temperatures, so that precious materials can be gathered. For Isaac, the years 1665–67 were a crucible. Unable to continue working at Cambridge, he went back to Woolsthorpe, where his genius was unleashed. The precious material that resulted was a new understanding of the world.

Right: Death stalks the land, as city dwellers flee the plague and carry the infection with them. There were repeated outbreaks of the plague in Europe during the 17th century.

These years of Newton's life are sometimes known in Latin as *anni mirabiles*, meaning "marvelous years." However, they occurred at the same time as two national disasters. In June 1665, the bubonic plague broke out in London. It was a terrible, deadly disease, which was spread by rat fleas, although no one knew that yet. As the plague spread out into the countryside, there was panic. Cambridge University was closed. By October, 70,000 people had died in the capital alone.

Isaac had nowhere to go but home. He rode north to Woolsthorpe Manor that August. He remained there until March 1666, when he returned briefly to Cambridge, before taking refuge at Woolsthorpe again until April 1667.

April 1665
Isaac Newton earns a Bachelor of Arts degree.

May 1665
Isaac considers tangents and the orbits of planets.

Freed from examinations and the irritating company of other students, Isaac was able to think creatively and to experiment. He made brilliant advances in mathematics and the science of physics.

On September 2, 1666, a second disaster struck London: the Great Fire broke out in the city. Londoners took to boats on the River Thames to escape the heat. By the time the fire had burned out four days later, it had destroyed some 13,200 homes, 89 churches, and St. Paul's Cathedral. About 100,000 people were made homeless, and an unknown number were killed. Much of the old medieval city lay in ruins. It was time to build a new city.

A blessing in disguise

The Great Fire of London in 1666 was a disaster, but it also brought some benefits. It destroyed many of the city's old rat-infested houses. The plague finally came to an end in December 1666.

Below: London burns in the Great Fire of 1666. The old St. Paul's Cathedral stands silhouetted against the flames.

June 7, 1665
The first reports of the plague in London are heard.

August 1665
Isaac Newton leaves Cambridge and seeks refuge from the plague at Woolsthorpe Manor.

As a "natural philosopher," Isaac Newton tried to understand more about the universe. His aim, as was the case with many other scientists in that age, was a religious one. He wanted to shed light on the wonders of God. However, the more he followed the demands of science, the more his beliefs differed from the traditional teachings of the churches.

Mathematics was Newton's great love. It was not some abstract notion to him, but a practical tool that could explain how things worked or why things happened. In February 1665, Isaac had developed the "binomial theorem." This was a clever use of algebra to work out logarithms with a great degree of accuracy. Logarithms are tables of figures that make it easier to do very complicated sums. Logarithmic tables were very useful in the days before electronic calculators.

Three months later, Newton was studying orbits, the paths taken by planets as they circle the sun. He tried to find a way of describing their course in mathematical terms. He decided that this could be done by considering the curved path in terms of a series of tangents. In geometry, a tangent is the point at which a straight line touches a curve.

Isaac was fascinated by the way in which a straight line might be broken down into a series of tinier and tinier lines and eventually become a curve.

A very secretive man

Isaac Newton filled notebooks with pages of figures and diagrams, but he tended to keep his discoveries to himself. This led to quarrels with other mathematicians later in his life. The great German mathematician Gottfried Leibniz (1646–1716) claimed to have invented calculus first.

1665

Robert Hooke's *Micrographia* is published. It reveals that plants are made of tiny cells.

September 1665

Isaac Newton is said to have seen an apple fall, arousing his interest in the force of gravity.

Starting in November 1665, he spent three years working out a system for calculating ever smaller measurements. He called it "fluxions," but we know it as "calculus." This combines arithmetic with geometry and algebra to compare the rate of change in one thing to the rate of change in another. For example, it can compare distance traveled with time taken, to show changes in speed. Calculus can be used to work out the length of curved lines or the area of irregular shapes.

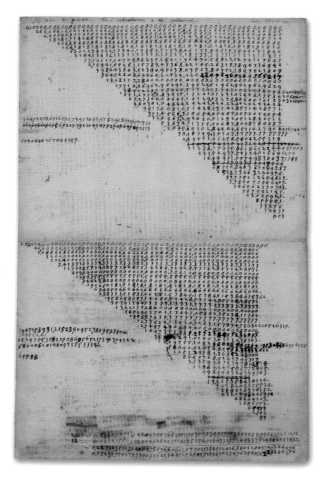

Above: No calculators or computers were available in Newton's day. Isaac Newton used brainpower to make calculations of up to 55 decimal places. He was fascinated by infinity, by the idea of things going on forever. He puzzled over the notion of a number being endlessly broken down into fractions without ever reaching zero.

Counting with pebbles

The name "calculus" comes from the Latin word for "pebble." The Greeks and Romans used pebbles for counting. The complicated system of calculation devised by Isaac Newton was not quite as simple!

November 1665

Newton starts to work on mathematical problems he calls "fluxions" (calculus).

March 20, 1666

Isaac Newton returns to Cambridge for a few months.

New Science

Above: This was Newton's diagram of his dangerous eye-ball experiment.

The branch of science that we call physics was at the heart of Isaac Newton's inquiries as a young man. Isaac was fascinated by what he decided must be the tiniest particles of matter, called atoms. He also carried out a series of experiments to discover the nature of light itself.

Isaac Newton knew the ideas on "atomism" of the Cambridge philosopher Henry More (1614–87), who had been born in Grantham. He also read the atomic theory of the French scientist Pierre Gassendi (1592–1655). Isaac decided that atoms must exist as the smallest, indivisible particles of matter, so tiny that they could not be seen. It was not until 1897 that the English physicist J.J. Thomson discovered that atoms contained even smaller particles, which he called electrons. Later scientists discovered that atoms also contained other particles, including protons and neutrons.

But what was light? We know now that it is energy that travels in waves. Newton believed it was made of particles. In fact, a modern theory of physics called "quantum theory" shows that he was partly correct.

1666
Isaac Newton works with prisms to examine the nature of light.

1666
Newton continues to develop his theories of gravity.

Seeing red

Isaac Newton's favorite color throughout his life was crimson. Whenever possible he had his room furnished with crimson curtains, crimson upholstery, and crimson cushions.

René Descartes believed light was some kind of pressure and that colors were a mixture of light and darkness. Newton was not convinced. He tried some very dangerous experiments. He poked a bodkin (a kind of blunt needle) behind his eye to see what would happen, and described the colors that he saw. He also tried staring at the sun, as it appeared reflected in a mirror. He was lucky not to be blinded and afterwards had to spend three days in a darkened room.

A less dangerous experiment was carried out using a prism, a triangle of glass that he had bought at Stourbridge fair, near Cambridge. When the sun shone through it, the prism gave off a range of colors. Isaac realized that white light was actually made up of all these different colors. When light was bent (or "refracted") by the prism, the separate colors became visible. The same effect is created as a rainbow, when sunlight is scattered through the natural prism of a raindrop. Isaac's discovery was a very important breakthrough in the understanding of light.

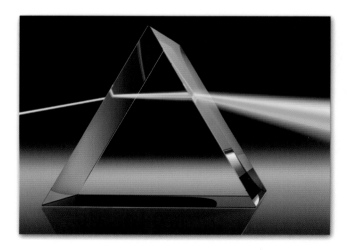

Right: A photograph reveals how a ray of light is refracted as it passes through a glass prism and is split into separate colors: violet, indigo, blue, green, yellow, orange, and red. This range of colors is known as the "spectrum."

June 1666
The plague flares up again. Isaac returns to Woolsthorpe.

July 1666
Naval battles take place between the Dutch and the English.

One late summer day, Isaac Newton was sitting in the orchard at Woolsthorpe Manor when an apple falling from a branch startled him. It set him thinking about gravity, the force that pulls objects toward the Earth. At least, that is how the story was told many years later. The legendary apple became one of the most famous fruits in history.

Isaac must have considered the question of gravity before. He had studied the work of Galileo and Kepler about gravity. But perhaps the fall of the apple really did set him thinking again. Gravity would occupy his mind for the next 20 years, while he worked on and perfected his theories.

Left: The peace of the Lincolnshire countryside was inspirational during the plague years. An apple tree growing at Woolsthorpe Manor today is said to be the descendant of a tree that grew there in Isaac Newton's lifetime and survived until 1820.

September 2, 1666

The Great Fire breaks out in Pudding Lane, London.

September 6, 1666

The Great Fire burns itself out. St. Paul's Cathedral has been destroyed.

"And the same year [1665] I began to think of gravity extending to ye orb of the Moon... & thereby computed the force requisite to keep the Moon in her orb with the force of gravity at the surface of the Earth, & found them answer pretty nearly. All this was in the two plague years of 1665–1666. For in those days I was in the prime of my age for invention & minded mathematicks and philosophy more than at any time since."

Isaac Newton recalls the Woolsthorpe years

If the Earth's gravity pulled the apple downward, why was the moon not pulled down to Earth as well? Newton took a step back from the problem and asked himself another question. Why did the moon not fly away into space? Perhaps it was held in orbit around the Earth by the force of gravity? This was the first time that anyone had wondered if gravity might govern the planets as well as objects on the Earth. Like a ball attached to a string and whirled around one's head, the moon could not escape. The reason it did not crash downward like an apple was that, at that distance, the force of gravity was weaker than it was on the Earth's surface.

By April 1667, it was time for Isaac to leave Woolsthorpe. Cambridge University was at last returning to business after the plague years. Isaac's mother gave him some money, and he headed south to the university once again. Isaac's months of refuge in the countryside had been well spent. Although few people had yet heard of this young Cambridge scholar, he was already the leading scientist, or "natural philosopher," of his day.

December 1666
The plague at last comes to an end in London.

April 1667
Isaac Newton returns to Cambridge University.

SECRETS OF THE
UNIVERSE

3

The Academic Life

Isaac Newton was back in Cambridge. During the summer of 1667, he relaxed and enjoyed himself, for probably the first time in his life. He played cards and visited taverns. He also began to think about the next steps in his career.

Isaac needed to become a junior fellow of Trinity College, so that he could receive an income and be given a free room at the college. This was a hurdle, as one often needed political influence or friends in high places to succeed. As a student, Isaac had only been a subsizar, but he did have a contact called Humphrey Babington. Babington was a relative of the Clarks of Grantham and had been made a senior fellow that year.

In September 1667, Isaac was tested in his studies. The election of junior fellows followed in October, and Newton was successful. The following year he was made a senior fellow and received his Master of Arts degree.

Isaac's work caught the attention of Isaac Barrow (1630–77), who since 1664 had been the Lucasian Professor of Mathematics at Cambridge. Barrow was impressed by the younger man's abilities, and this led to Newton being offered the job of Lucasian Professor himself in 1669, after Barrow resigned.

Above: On returning to Cambridge, Isaac Newton had to buy the correct academic dress for a Bachelor of Arts in the university. It included a cap, gown, and hood.

Previous page: Isaac Newton made this fine telescope in 1668.

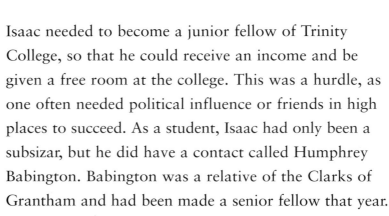

October 2, 1667
Isaac Newton is elected a junior fellow of Trinity College. He becomes a senior fellow on March 16, 1668.

February 1668
Newton works on a new telescope design.

A Lucasian Professor

The Lucasian Chair of Mathematics at Cambridge University was named after Henry Lucas, who set up the post in 1664. Famous Lucasian professors after Newton included Charles Babbage, inventor of calculating machines, and the black hole expert Stephen Hawking.

Below: Newton's work table is recreated at Trinity College. The instruments on the table include a prism for splitting light, an astrolabe for studying the stars, and tables of logarithms.

Normally Newton would have had to become a priest to qualify. At first he agreed, but he kept putting the decision off. His secret reason was that he could no longer accept the Christian belief in the Trinity, which stated that God's identity was threefold—as Father, Son, and Holy Spirit. In 1675, the university decided that Newton did not have to become a priest, and he took up the position of Lucasian Professor.

August 5, 1668
Isaac Newton makes his first visit to London.

October 29, 1669
Newton is elected Lucasian Professor of Mathematics. He takes up the position in 1675.

Jars and Telescopes

In his new post as Lucasian Professor of Mathematics, Isaac Newton was not a great communicator. He was expected to give lectures, but few students attended. That was quite common in Cambridge at that period. Newton was, in fact, rather distracted from mathematics for a time by a new passion—alchemy.

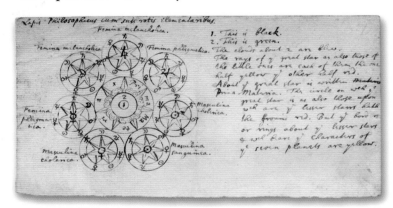

Left: Newton himself sketched a copy of this symbolic diagram of the mysterious "philosopher's stone." For the genius who discovered so much, this was a piece of research that led nowhere.

Alchemy was an early version of chemistry, but it was more mystical than scientific. Its aim was a symbolic union between the individual and the universe. The universe was believed to contain materials or principles that were opposed and yet needed each other—for example, earth and air, fire and water. The most perfect union of substances was believed to be gold, which was seen as a symbol of God. Alchemists were obsessed with turning non-precious metals into gold—often not for spiritual reasons, but in order to make their fortune. Needless to say, alchemy became mixed up with all sorts of tricks and frauds. Alchemists were even suspected of being in league with the devil.

1669
Isaac Newton conducts methodical experiments in alchemy.

1669
A German alchemist named Hennig Brandt discovers phosphorus while seeking the "philosopher's stone."

Amid all this hocus-pocus, alchemists were doing some useful work in experimenting with metals and other substances, and were discovering more about them. If every substance was made up of tiny atoms, then surely it was not so far-fetched to believe that it might be possible to rearrange them and so change one metal into another, and a base metal such as lead into gold? Many great scientists were interested in alchemy. Robert Boyle (1627–91), the Irish scientist regarded as the father of modern chemistry, was an alchemist.

It was hardly surprising, therefore, that Isaac Newton began to carry out alchemical experiments in the late 1660s. One story has it that, while carrying out an experiment in 1677, Isaac blew up his rooms at Cambridge and started a fire!

Isaac wrote to other alchemists, but always in secret. He did not want to be accused of black magic or other religious crimes.

Above: A 1652 drawing shows the laboratory of an alchemist, with crucibles, furnaces, and jars.

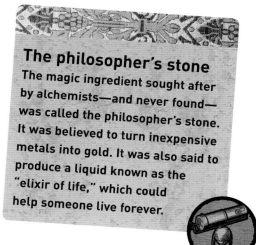

The philosopher's stone
The magic ingredient sought after by alchemists—and never found—was called the philosopher's stone. It was believed to turn inexpensive metals into gold. It was also said to produce a liquid known as the "elixir of life," which could help someone live forever.

November 1669
Michelangelo is commissioned by Pope Paul III to remodel the buildings on Rome's Capitoline Hill.

1670
The rebuilding of London begins under the direction of architect Christopher Wren.

Handmade

Isaac Newton had not lost the practical skills he had shown as a child. Every part of his new reflecting telescope was made by his own hand. He made the fittings and polished the mirrors.

Isaac Newton's interest in alchemy was that of an idealist with a curious, open mind, rather than someone who wanted to dabble in magic. Indeed, it was Newton who finally brought in the scientific age which chased away superstition. At this time, he was perfecting a more practical device for investigating the secrets of the universe. It was called the reflecting telescope.

The refracting telescope had been the first type of telescope to be invented, by the Dutch spectacle-maker Hans Lippershey (died c. 1619), in 1608. It was greatly improved by Galileo in 1610 and is still in use today. Light enters a tube and passes through a concave (inward-curving) lens, which bends or refracts the light and so brings an image into focus. This image is then magnified by a second lens, in the eyepiece.

Other scientists had tried to improve telescope design. In 1663, the Scottish mathematician James Gregory (1638–75) had worked out that mirrors could be used to produce a clearer image. It was Robert Hooke (1635–1703) who made the first reflecting telescope, using it to make new discoveries in the night sky. However, it was Newton who designed and built by far the best one, in February 1668. It could magnify distant objects by as much as 40 times. Light entering the tube was reflected from a concave mirror back to a flat mirror, which was set at an angle of 45 degrees. This beamed an image into the eyepiece, where it was magnified by lenses.

January 1670

Isaac Newton gives his first lecture on optics.

December 1671

Newton's reflecting telescope is demonstrated to the Royal Society. He is proposed as a member.

In 1671, Isaac's telescope was shown to the Royal Society, the association of Britain's most distinguished scientists, and to King Charles II himself. A report was sent to the Dutch scientist Christiaan Huygens (1629–95), the great expert on optics (the science of light and vision), as it was customary for leading scientists to exchange reports.

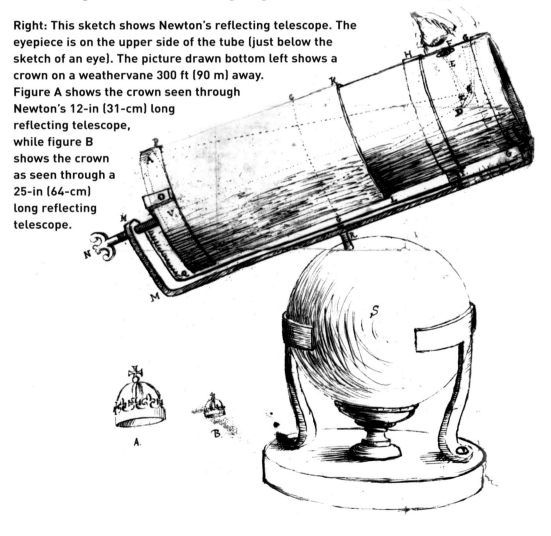

Right: This sketch shows Newton's reflecting telescope. The eyepiece is on the upper side of the tube (just below the sketch of an eye). The picture drawn bottom left shows a crown on a weathervane 300 ft (90 m) away. Figure A shows the crown seen through Newton's 12-in (31-cm) long reflecting telescope, while figure B shows the crown as seen through a 25-in (64-cm) long reflecting telescope.

January 11, 1672

Isaac Newton is elected to the Royal Society.

February 8, 1672

Newton sends a letter on light and color to the Royal Society. It is criticized by Robert Hooke.

The Royal Society

In the 1640s, a group of natural philosophers and mathematicians began to meet in London, to have discussions and compare notes. They had close contact with other natural philosophers who used to meet at Wadham College, Oxford. From 1659 onward, they held meetings at Gresham College in London. In 1660, they founded the "Royal Society" as an official academy of the sciences, and it was given a royal charter in 1662. One of its leading members was the great physicist and chemist Robert Boyle. Its first director of experiments was Robert Hooke. In 1671, the astronomer Seth Ward (1617–89) proposed Isaac Newton for membership, and he was elected in January 1672. However, Newton and Hooke never liked each other and often quarreled. Hooke was argumentative and Newton was too easily offended.

Left: The Royal Society prided itself on original research. It believed in experiment and proof and took nothing for granted. This early microscope was designed by Robert Hooke, a leading member of the Royal Society. Hooke was a brilliant physicist, astronomer, inventor, and architect.

Right: Isaac Newton was elected to the council of the Royal Society in 1699 and became president on November 30, 1703. This later picture shows Newton (center) at a meeting.

SIR,

THESE are to give Notice, That on *Monday* the First Day of *December* 1712, (being the next after St. *ANDREW's DAY*) the Council and Officers of the ROYAL SOCIETY are to be Elected for the Year ensuing; at which ELECTION your Presence is expected, at Nine of the Clock in the Forenoon, at the House of the ROYAL SOCIETY, in *Crane Court*, *Fleet Street.*

To
Thomas Jssed Efq.

Js. Newton P.R.S.

Left: Isaac Newton's signature as president appears on this notice of elections to the Royal Society in 1712. Over the years, some of the most famous names in the history of science would be elected as fellows of the Royal Society.

Below: The Royal Society had various homes in London. This is Crane Court, which became its headquarters in 1710, during the presidency of Isaac Newton.

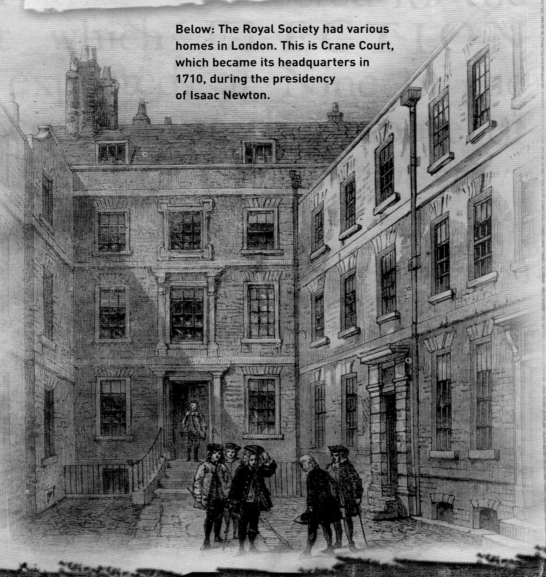

Comets' Tails

In 1679, Isaac's mother Hannah died of a fever. He had to return to Woolsthorpe Manor from Cambridge to sort out family affairs. Isaac was now 37 years old and a respected member of the Royal Society.

Isaac's mind was occupied with astronomy at this time. Between 1679 and 1680, he exchanged letters with Robert Hooke about the movement of the planets. Newton also observed comets in the night sky. Comets are balls of rock, dust, and ice which produce a long tail as they approach the sun. In ancient times, people thought comets were warnings of disasters or important events. In Newton's day, people had little idea of what comets were or how they moved. Some scientists, such as Christiaan Huygens, believed that comets moved in a straight line. However, Robert Hooke and the Italian astronomer Giovanni Cassini (1625–1712) believed that comets follow a curved orbit around the sun.

Left: In 1684, Newton exchanged ideas about gravity and planetary motion with Robert Hooke, Edmond Halley, and the great architect Christopher Wren. Newton later prepared a series of papers known in Latin as *De Motu Corporum in Gyrum* ("About the Motion of Orbiting Bodies").

1680–81
Isaac Newton observes comets in the night sky.

January 1684
Newton, Halley, Hooke, and Wren exchange ideas about gravity and planetary motion.

Left: The new observatory at Greenwich, beside the River Thames, was directed by John Flamsteed, Britain's first Astronomer Royal.

In 1684–85 Newton made calculations which showed that the path of the comet that appeared in the night sky in 1680 was indeed curved.

Newton thought that comets might serve a function in space, such as renewing the sun's fuel. He was mistaken, but his calculations later made it possible for English astronomer Edmond Halley (1656–1742) to predict—correctly—that a comet he observed in 1682 would reappear in 1758–59 in the course of its orbit. Newton's calculations on orbits also disproved a belief that a gas called "ether" filled the universe. He showed that planets move through space without being slowed down by any such substance.

Newton was able to carry out his ongoing work on planets, the moon, and orbits thanks to the meticulous work of astronomer John Flamsteed (1646–1719). However, Newton accused Flamsteed of being slow to complete his calculations and delaying Newton's own work.

The coffee craze

Newton was an occasional visitor to London in the 1680s. The most fashionable places to be seen were coffeehouses. It was there that businessmen and politicians made deals or exchanged gossip and news. Some historians say that Newton and his colleagues sometimes met in coffeehouses to discuss scientific ideas.

November 1684

Newton's essay *De Motu* is received by the Royal Society.

December 1684

Gottfried Leibniz publishes his theory of calculus in *Novus Methodus* ("New Method").

MAN OF THE
WORLD

4

The *Principia*

In 1686, some twenty years after Isaac Newton's greatest period of creative thinking, his theories were at last refined and perfected to the point where they could be published. The great work was called *Principia Mathematica* and was published in three volumes. Its full title in English meant the "Mathematical Principles of Natural Philosophy."

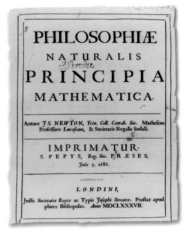

Above: In April 1686, the first volume of *Principia* was presented to the Royal Society. The other volumes were printed the next year.

Previous page: A "frost fair" is held in London, on the frozen River Thames, around the time that Newton arrived in the city.

Newton's aim was to describe universal laws of motion which underpin the forces of nature. Why and how do things move? What makes them speed up or slow down and come to a halt? Newton's answer came in three parts.

The first law of motion states that an object that is moving steadily will remain in that same state until force is applied to it. Today, we know that a spacecraft could move through space forever, unless affected by the pull of gravity, or slowed down by a planet's atmosphere. Likewise, an object that is not moving tends to remain motionless, until an outside force is applied to it.

The second law of motion states that the acceleration of an object depends on two things—the object's mass and the force acting upon it. As the force increases, so does the acceleration.

February 6, 1685
King Charles II dies. His brother James II of England (James VII of Scotland) takes his place.

1686
Edmond Halley publishes the world's first meteorological, or weather, chart.

However, if the mass of the object increases, the object will slow down. Newton expresses this relationship as an equation, in which the force is called "F," the mass of the object is "m," and the acceleration is "a." The relationship between them can be summed up as "F=ma"—the applied force is equal to mass times the acceleration.

Newton's third law of motion states that for every action there is an equal and opposite reaction—a swimmer pushes against the water; the water pushes against the swimmer.

In the third volume of *Principia*, Newton finalized his understanding of gravity. He stated that every object in the universe attracts every other object. The force of attraction, known as gravity, lies between the centers of each object. The strength of gravitational force is determined by the mass of the two objects and the distance between them.

Ruffled feathers

The publication of *Principia* almost never took place. Hooke complained that he should have been credited in the book for his work on gravity. Newton was enraged. It was Halley who calmed both men down and ensured that the book was finally printed.

Right: By the age of 46, when this portrait was painted, Isaac was widely recognized as a genius. Across Europe, his work was hailed as a historic achievement.

1686–87
Principia Mathematica is presented to the Royal Society in three volumes, and published with the help of Halley.

1688
Britain's Glorious Revolution: William of Orange is invited to become king.

Friends and Foes

Above: A Swiss mathematician called Nicholas Fatio de Duillier (1664–1753) was one of the few close friends Isaac Newton ever had. They first met in 1689, when Fatio was a fellow of the Royal Society. Fatio was an emotional and rather boastful young man. Fatio and Newton's friendship was broken off in 1693, and this may have brought on Newton's depression.

The publication of the *Principia* was the high point of Isaac Newton's scientific career. But as endless quarrels with Robert Hooke showed, he was increasingly irritable and angry. Periods of rage sometimes spurred him on to more creative thinking, but more often he sank back into periods of black despair.

Isaac often felt ill. In fact, he had spent much of his life imagining that he had one illness or another. In 1693, he suffered what today we might call a nervous breakdown, a period of severe depression.

Isaac Newton had few doubts about his own scientific genius. Indeed, he often seemed arrogant. However, he was forever nervous that his unusual views on religion and alchemy would be discovered. Perhaps the problem went even deeper. Something had gnawed away at Isaac's inner happiness and security ever since he was a child. He was often quick to take offense.

December 23, 1688

King James II flees to France, leaving his son-in-law and daughter, William of Orange and Mary, to take the throne.

1689

Isaac Newton meets Nicholas Fatio de Duillier and also the philosopher John Locke.

Isaac's assistant Humphrey Newton (no relation), who was hired in 1683–4, said that he only saw his employer laugh once—and that was about geometry.

Isaac Newton did have some allies who helped him forward through this difficult period. John Locke, the great English philosopher (1632–1704), greatly admired Newton's scientific methods and became a friend. Samuel Pepys (1633–1703) was another. President of the Royal Society for a time, Pepys is now more famous for his secret diaries of London life in the 1660s. The great architect Christopher Wren (1632–1723) also knew Newton well and was a leading figure in the Royal Society.

Below: Sir Christopher Wren's masterpiece was the new St. Paul's Cathedral, built between 1675 and 1710. Wren set about rebuilding much of London after the Great Fire of 1666.

January 1692
Isaac Newton attends Robert Boyle's funeral in London.

July 1693
Isaac Newton has a severe nervous breakdown.

London Life

In the 17th century, Cambridge University was considered to be such an important institution that it sent its own representative to the English Parliament, in London. In 1689, Isaac Newton was chosen to be its member of Parliament.

Newton served as a member of Parliament for a year. He reported back to Cambridge, but made no speeches in Parliament himself. The new post did mean that he now had to spend much more time in London. Prodded on by friends such as Locke, he began to make useful social contacts.

He soon became something of a celebrity in fashionable circles and, even more remarkably, found that he rather enjoyed it. In 1689, he was asked to dine with the new king, William III. He was befriended by other powerful people at the royal court, such as Charles Mordaunt, Earl of Monmouth, and by Sir Francis and Lady Masham.

Right: A plate celebrates the reign of William III and Mary II. Mary was the Protestant daughter of the Catholic ruler James II of England (VII of Scotland). When James fled the country, Mary and her husband, the Dutchman William of Orange, were invited to rule jointly in his place, starting in 1689.

March 1696
Isaac Newton becomes Warden of the Royal Mint.

April 1696
Newton moves to London to take up his new duties.

Right: An 18th-century French illustration shows coins being made in a mint. In Newton's day, the English Royal Mint was based in the Tower of London.

Charles Montagu, Earl of Halifax, who had been at college with Isaac, now controlled the nation's finances as Chancellor of the Exchequer.

In March 1696, Isaac Newton was made Warden of the Royal Mint, where coins were manufactured. He was not expected to do much real work, as the post was intended as a personal favor or honor. However, Newton took the job very seriously and oversaw the introduction of new coins, designed to be harder to forge, or counterfeit, than the old ones.

In April 1696, Newton decided to move to London, and that August he made his home on Jermyn Street. It was probably then that Catherine Barton moved in. She was the daughter of his half-sister Hannah, and she acted as his housekeeper. Although Newton was still Lucasian Professor at Cambridge, in 1699 he was given a new title as Master of the Royal Mint. Isaac Newton, the man with his head in the stars, had become a man of the world.

Hunting down forgers

In the 17th century, forgery was common, and many coins were fakes or had valuable metal clipped off them. During his time at the Royal Mint, Isaac Newton cracked down on the forgers, bringing many to justice and seeing them hanged.

August 1696
Isaac Newton sets up a new home on Jermyn Street, London.

January 1697
Gottfried Leibniz and Johann Bernoulli set a difficult mathematical problem which Newton solves overnight.

Isaac Newton was honored overseas as well as in his own country. In 1699, he was made an associate of the French Académie des Sciences. However, at home and abroad some scientists were jealous of him, and a few were openly critical. Although he may have been more confident in London's high society, he was as touchy as ever when it came to his life's work. He was often petty and unforgiving toward his critics.

In November 1701, Isaac was elected to serve another term as the member of Parliament for Cambridge University. The following month, he resigned as Lucasian Professor. In 1702, King William III died in a riding accident. Since William's wife Mary II had already died, his sister-in-law Anne became queen.

March 1703 brought news of another death, that of Newton's old foe Robert Hooke.

Right: This portrait shows Isaac Newton in 1703 at the age of 60. It was painted by Charles Jervas, and was presented to the Royal Society in 1717.

December 10, 1701
Isaac Newton resigns as Lucasian Professor of Mathematics at Cambridge.

November 30, 1703
Newton is elected president of the Royal Society.

This left the way clear for Isaac to be elected president of the Royal Society at last. He ran the organization with great efficiency. Newton also felt that he could now release his work on light without Hooke's objections ringing in his ears— Hooke had disputed Newton's findings on the spectrum for many years. *Opticks* was published, unusually, in an English edition as well as a Latin edition, in 1704. Newton's account of calculus, called *Fluxions*, was also printed. This immediately set him at odds with the German mathematician Gottfried Leibniz. The dispute over who had first discovered calculus would rumble on, until Leibniz's death in 1716.

In 1705, Isaac was awarded a great public honor when he was knighted by Queen Anne. He was now Sir Isaac Newton. He was wealthy, with a fine London house and servants. His pretty, intelligent niece was courted by the rich and famous. Isaac Newton had come a long way since his childhood on a Lincolnshire farm.

Above: In 1710, Sir Isaac Newton moved to this house near London's Leicester Square, and he lived here until 1725. The building is shown in about 1812, when it was being used as a Sunday school.

The bigwigs

Today we still use the word "bigwigs" to describe important people. The term dates back to the late 1600s and early 1700s, when the French fashion of long, full wigs was taken up in London by men of high social standing. Paintings of Newton in his later years show him in such a wig.

February 1704
Newton publishes the first edition of *Opticks*.

April 16, 1705
Isaac Newton is knighted by Queen Anne in Cambridge.

"All Was Light"

Above: Newton's legacy did not impress everyone. The poet and artist William Blake (1757–1827) believed that the scientific age ignored human imagination and dreams. Blake's painting of 1795 shows Isaac Newton grimly measuring out the universe and staring fixedly down at his own diagrams.

The 18th century is sometimes called the "Age of Reason" or "the Enlightenment." It marks the start of the modern world, of scientific advance and understanding. Although Newton belonged to the older generation of natural philosophers, he did more than any other scientist to bring in this new way of thinking. The part Newton played was widely recognized in the years after his death. In 1730, the English poet Alexander Pope (1688–1744) wrote:

"Nature, and Nature's Laws
lay hid in night,
God said, Let Newton be!
and all was light."

The light of Newton's breakthroughs shone down the centuries and brought forward an astonishing range of scientific discoveries, inventions, and theories. Newton is still being honored in many different ways. The "newton," a unit of measurement for force, is named after him.

Left: Albert Einstein (1879–1955) shared Isaac Newton's fascination with gravity, light, motion, and the universe. However, he realized that Newton's laws were not as fixed as everyone had believed. Einstein showed that time and motion do not work according to unchanging laws. They may vary according to the speed at which one is traveling. This theory was called "relativity."

Left: Earth rises over the horizon of the moon, as seen from the command module of the spacecraft Apollo 12 in November 1969. Without Isaac Newton's discoveries about gravity, space travel would have been impossible.

Left: A cluster of domes makes up the Isaac Newton Group of Telescopes (known as ING), which began operating in 1984. They are sited on La Palma, one of the Canary Islands, in Spain.

Active to the End

As Isaac grew older, he spent time reading ancient history and the Bible. He was trying to work out a timescale of human history, but it proved too large a task. Despite his failing health, he continued with his public duties.

Above: This portrait shows Isaac Newton at the age of 82. To the end, he tried to keep up his duties at the Royal Mint and the Royal Society.

In London, the talk in those days was of politics and money. Isaac was very rich and he often showed generosity toward needy relatives. In a big financial crash of 1720, known as the "South Sea Bubble," Newton lost as much as £20,000 (worth about $4.5 million today)—a vast fortune at that time—yet he still remained very wealthy. He exclaimed that he could calculate the motions of heavenly bodies, but not the madness of people when it came to money.

In 1725, John Conduitt, who had married Isaac's niece Catherine, began to write down the old man's memoirs. Isaac was now 82 years old. These are the stories of his life that have survived, and it is hard to tell whether all of them are true or not. At about this time, Isaac's health began to decline. He suffered from all sorts of ailments, including kidney stones, gout, and inflammation of the lungs. He ate lightly, usually just broth, and sometimes had to use a wheelchair.

November 14, 1716
Gottfried Leibniz, Newton's old rival, dies.

1725
Newton relates his memoirs to John Conduitt, husband of Catherine Barton.

"I know not what I appear to the world, but to myself I seem to have been only like a boy playing on the sea-shore, and diverting myself in now and then finding a smoother pebble or a prettier shell, whilst the great ocean of truth lay all undiscovered before me."

Isaac Newton

Early in 1727, Isaac burned many of his personal papers, aware that he could not live much longer. These papers may have been notes on alchemy or material about his private life—Newton was a very secretive man. He died in the early hours of March 20, 1727, in the London district of Kensington, where he had lived for the last two years of his life.

On March 28, Newton's body lay in state in London's Westminster Abbey, an honor given only to people considered very important. At his funeral on April 4, the coffin of this Lincolnshire farm boy was carried by dukes and earls, and followed to the grave by leading fellows of the Royal Society. It was like a royal funeral, said some—and all for a scientist! This surely was a new age.

Right: An ornate monument to Sir Isaac Newton was placed in Westminster Abbey in 1731. Its inscription, in Latin, ends: "Mortals rejoice that there has existed such and so great an ornament of the human race."

March 20, 1727

Sir Isaac Newton dies at his home in Kensington, London.

April 4, 1727

A state funeral for Sir Isaac Newton takes place in Westminster Abbey, London.

Glossary

acceleration an increase in speed.

alchemy non-scientific practices once carried out in the hope of transforming base metals, such as lead, into gold.

algebra the study of mathematical relationships using letters and symbols.

apothecary an old-fashioned word for a pharmacist.

astronomer somebody who studies the planets, moons, stars, and the workings of the universe.

atom in Newton's day, the term given to the tiniest possible particle of matter. Today, we know that atoms are made up of even smaller parts.

bachelor's degree a first degree, or course of study, at a university.

binomial in algebra, a two-part sum such as "2x + 3y."

binomial theorem a formula which gives the power of any binomial without multiplying out each sum in full.

calculus systems of mathematics which use tiny measurements to compare one rate of change with that of another.

Catholic a follower of the Catholic Church based in Rome.

chemistry the scientific investigation of what things are made of and how substances react with each other.

comet a ball of dust and ice that travels around the sun. It develops a long tail of gas and dust as it nears the sun.

Commonwealth the name of the English republican government from 1649 to 1660.

crucible (a) a dish or part of a furnace used to melt metals (b) a testing time that may lead to a great change.

elixir of life a mythical potion which allows one to live forever.

ether (a) an imaginary medium once believed to fill all space and to enable the transmission of light and heat (b) an inflammable, colorless liquid.

fluxions Isaac Newton's name for calculus.

geometry a branch of mathematics which is concerned with shape and form.

grammar school a type of boy's school common in English towns during the lifetime of Isaac Newton. It provided an education, often free or inexpensively, based on the study of Latin grammar.

gravity the attraction which pulls one body toward another, as when an apple falls to the ground.

law a scientific principle or truth, based upon a relation or sequence, and which never varies.

logarithm the power by which a fixed number (the "base") must be raised in order to produce a given number.

Lord Protector the title of the English head of state during the period of republican rule known as the Protectorate (1653–59). Holders of the title were Oliver Cromwell and Richard Cromwell.

mint an official site for the manufacture of money.

monarchy a form of government based on rule by a single person, such as a king.

natural philosophy in the lifetime of Isaac Newton, this was the name given to what we would now call science.

optics the branch of physics that deals with light and vision.

orbit the path of one object around another, as when a planet travels around the sun, or a moon travels around a planet.

Parliamentarian a supporter of the English Parliament against the king during the English Civil War.

philosopher someone who studies knowledge, truth, and logic.

philosopher's stone a mythical substance which alchemists believed could turn metals of little value into gold.

physics the branch of science which is concerned with the nature of objects and how they behave, investigating such matters as motion and force.

prism a transparent object, generally with a triangular base, which refracts and reflects rays of light.

Protestant any of the Christian individuals, groups, or churches which do not recognize the authority of the Catholic Church.

Puritan a Protestant of the 17th century who called for further religious reform and simpler forms of worship.

quantum theory a theory developed in the 20th century, which states that changes of energy such as those taking place in atoms, are not continuous but are made up of separate bursts of energy, known as quanta.

reflecting telescope a telescope that uses mirrors rather than lenses to form an image.

refract to change the direction of a ray of light or heat.

refracting telescope a telescope that uses lenses rather than mirrors to form an image.

relativity the principle that all motion we observe is relative rather than absolute.

republic a state which has no monarch, generally one with a system of government which represents the people.

Restoration the return of the monarchy to Britain in 1660.

Royalist a supporter of King Charles I in the English Civil War.

spectrum the full range of colors.

subsizar in Cambridge University during Isaac Newton's lifetime, this was a class of undergraduates who had to perform services for other students and for fellows in order to pay for their upkeep and tuition.

tangent a touching point in geometry, as where a straight line meets the circumference of a circle.

vortex (plural: vortices) a spinning movement of matter around a center.

Bibliography

Dead Famous: Isaac Newton and His Apple, Kjartan Poskitt, Scholastic Hippo, 1999

Isaac Newton, James Gleick, Harper Perennial, 2004

Isaac Newton, Kathleen Krull, Viking, 2006

Isaac Newton: The Last Sorceror, Michael White, Fourth Estate, 1998

Never at Rest: A Biography of Isaac Newton, Richard S. Westfall, Cambridge University Press, 1980

Sources of quotes:

p. 8 John Conduitt's memorandum of his conversation with Isaac Newton, Aug 31, 1726, Keynes MS 130.10

p. 17 Catherine Storer (later Mrs. Vincent), from p.45–6 of William Stukeley, *Memoirs of Sir Isaac Newton*, ed. A Hastings White, London, Taylor Francis, 1936

p. 33 Portsmouth papers, Additional MSS of Isaac Newton, Cambridge University Library

p. 56 Alexander Pope, "Epitaph Intended for Sir Isaac Newton in Westminster Abbey," 1730

p. 59 No. 1259 from Joseph Spence, *Observations, Anecdotes and Characters of Books and Men*, ed. J Osborn, Oxford University Press, 1966

Some Web sites that will help you to explore Isaac Newton's world:

www.newtonproject.ic.ac.uk
An ongoing project to create a searchable online catalog of all Newton's writings.

www.newton.cam.ac.uk/newton.html
Links to Newton resources on the Internet.

www.ing.iac.es
Web site of the Isaac Newton Group of telescopes.

Index